Tropical Living. Dream Houses in Punta Cana

Tropical Living

Dream Houses in Punta Cana

Edited by
Naty Abascal

Photography by
Guido Taroni

Foreword by
Anna Wintour

RIZZOLI
NEW YORK

New York · Paris · London · Milan

Contents

Foreword

I first met Oscar at a cocktail party in New York soon after I came to *American Vogue.* Oscar was extraordinary at the fine art of friendship, and so he and I instantly became the closest of friends. His wife Annette and I built our relationship more slowly—but it became just as important to me. Now she is as close as family, and part of the fabric of my life.

Being a friend of Oscar's (and there were legions of us) meant he threw open doors everywhere you went. That might be a chic dinner in New York, Paris, or London, where you might be seated next to a politician, or a baseball star, or you might be introduced to an actor you knew from TV, or an opera singer, or Spanish royalty—you never knew who you might meet!

Mornings typically started with an early phone call. "Dearest one," he'd say, "what are your plans today?" This meant he was cooking up something special to do that night. But nothing was more memorable than my annual visits to the Dominican Republic, the place Oscar most loved, and a whole country that loved him right back. First, there was the compound in La Romana, next to the airport, with the wicker furniture and a vaguely Polynesian air. Annette said it was like living on the runway, but the children loved it. Oscar took them swimming with the dolphins and planned incredible Easter egg hunts. There were always brilliant and surprising guests at each meal, sometimes forty in the house, which made for a wonderful stay (except, of course, that time Moises, Oscar's young son, put hot chili peppers in my daughter Bee's private stash of Oreos!).

Eventually, Annette prevailed and the family moved to Punta Cana, living in shacks on the beach while Oscar built a gift to his wife: the majestic and exquisite Villa Corales—their first real home together. I remember taking long walks with Annette through the jungle and out onto the beach—empty and magical—as Oscar's house rose in record time. Suddenly, it was finished, just in time for Christmas. Oscar sang and danced, and we felt welcomed and at home. And Annette and Oscar were married in their exquisite tiny chapel. From there Punta Cana grew and grew. Tennis camps, golf courses, and huge houses were built along the once-deserted beach that Annette and I had walked together. But everything had Oscar's touch, and whether we stayed at Villa Corales or in the wonderful guest villas at Tortuga Bay (where we were the very first visitors!), there was never a doubt about our Christmas plans. When Oscar left us, Annette kept the house just as he had—open to all. She was always the most gracious hostess, but when Covid hit, the house felt too big, too lonely. And one spring day I received a call. "I sold Corales," Annette told me.

I had told everyone we could never stay at Tortuga Bay again, but then Christmas came around and my friends and family asked for dates and we rented two houses there. That first time was hard—no Annette, no Oscar—and the property felt so empty.

But now we play at the Oscar de la Renta tennis courts with Felix, the amazing tennis coach, and I present a trophy in Oscar's honor. We visit the beautiful Villa Corales and the chapel, which remains exactly as Oscar and Annette left it. Annette had the wisdom to sell the house completely intact to Frank Ranieri and his family; Frank was Oscar's great friend and business partner. Like Oscar, the Ranieris are the most generous and gracious of hosts.

We often talk about all the amazing adventures we had over the years. Like the Christmas that my thirteen-year-old son, Charlie, complained about a stomach ache and Annette told him to toughen up. It turned out he had a ruptured appendix, and Oscar drove him through the night to the hospital, where he was operated on next to a cocaine mule whose stomach had burst. I always thought that was when Charlie decided to become a doctor.

Or the night Bee, age eleven, was asked to play cards with an ex-president, a famous mathematician, and Oscar—and she won!

Or the time I was asked to invite Cristiano Ronaldo for dinner, as I'd spotted him on the beach with an exceptionally beautiful girlfriend. As I drove them home after a long night, Cristiano said, "Well I have never had dinner with so many old people before! But it was actually quite fun."

Going back each holiday to Punta Cana honors Oscar, his love of life, his love for his friends—and for his beautiful country.

Anna Wintour

How It All Started
Prologue

Punta Cana came into my life one day through love, and it would become one of the great loves of my life. I met Frank Rainieri and we began seeing each other romantically, so my encounter with his great passion—Punta Cana—was imminent.

On that first trip, I discovered Frank's passion for Punta Cana, and I also understood that loving him meant loving this place. Frank spoke passionately about Punta Cana, describing what he would develop and where he would do each thing. "There will be a golf course there, a hotel there, all that will be a real estate development, a marina here," he told me. I, incredulous but in love, nodded at everything and said "Fantastic, wonderful." Today, I have to admit that everything Punta Cana embodies respects the master plan in Frank's head: everything he drew for me with his finger on the ground has been fulfilled.

It all started with a simple handshake when prominent American lawyer Theodore (Ted) W. Kheel and Frank decided to build some small cabins to turn the place into a tourist development. Ted—together with a group of important businessmen and trade union leaders—had bought a large piece of land in the middle of nowhere in an unknown (to them) country just because the price was right. More than ten years passed before we convinced Club Med to build in Punta Cana and with that, to open the area. Years later, after we already had a hotel and an airport, Frank received a strange call: it was Oscar de la Renta asking if he could come visit. Of course! Who would say no to Oscar de la Renta? He said he was coming with a friend, and he showed up with Julio Iglesias! That afternoon, after lunch, we went to see what is now Corales, and the van got stuck. It was very funny to see Oscar and Julio next to Frank, pushing the vehicle.

We had already started the Tortuga development and we had built several houses around the Tortuga Bay Hotel. We began the

Corales development with Oscar and Julio; the houses there, along with Ted's and ours, would be the first homes in Corales. This was followed by Arrecife and Hacienda, two magnificent projects that quickly became reality. Our latest real estate project, Lagos, is already under development.

Punta Cana has been our life, our dream, and our reality. And Ted, Oscar, and Julio, our perfect partners and dear friends. I firmly believe we have been God's instruments in developing this area. Today it is the country's main tourist hub, with more than 2,500 employees, and has the island's highest per capita income.

Our dream is not over. We keep wishing and working, now with our children at the head. We love Punta Cana and are dreaming just as much as day one.

Haydée Rainieri

Punta Cana An Eternal Love Story

To speak of Punta Cana is to speak of a very important person in my life: Oscar de la Renta. My first memory of the Dominican Republic goes back to New York in the 1960s. I had just arrived in the city to participate in the '64 World's Fair and Oscar was one of the first people I met. Our unswerving friendship endured until his passing in 2014.

In the early 1970s, Oscar began to build his home in La Romana (a place that became his refuge to escape the rigors of his successful fashion career). He called this house "Casa La Madre" [Mother House], and Oscar was enormously happy there.

But twenty years later (in the early 1990s) the air traffic in the area had become a nightmare—the landing strip was next to his house—and, in Oscar's opinion, the area was beginning to get too busy.

He had been wanting to move for a while. He was looking for something more isolated, farther from the social scene, which, just like in New York, was beginning to come alive in his native land, the Dominican Republic. It was becoming a desirable destination for the "happy few," who back then made up the true "jet set."

One day, accompanied by Julio Iglesias, he took a small plane and decided to fly over the island. When they reached the eastern end of it, they spotted a stretch of jungle shaped like an arrowhead. It had endless white-sand beaches and uniquely blue-green, clear waters. Punta Cana. This was the place. Punta Cana would be Oscar's new paradise.

They got in touch with the landowners, and thus began his (and my) new adventure in his native land. I say it was also my adventure because from then until I lost my dearest Oscar, this piece of land has been the scene of countless unique moments. The true protagonists of this story are the joy of living, music, light, food, dance (Oscar was a wonderful dancer!), the sea . . . but above all, its people and the constant flow of characters and situations we experienced "as a family."

I have watched the birth, creation, and development of Punta Cana and its Resort & Club. I have enjoyed it with my children. I have met incredible people who, many years later, I still call friends. All because of Oscar's magic and genius.

This was halfway through the 1990s, but in order to understand the journey this miracle in the heart of the Caribbean took, we must go back nearly three decades.

Oscar and Julio had contacted Frank Rainieri, director and developer of a project that, financed by Theodore W. Kheel and started in the late 1960s, would become one of the most successful urban adventures of the twentieth century.

A project that began in the most whimsical way imaginable (which at the beginning was little more than a few small bungalows) gave rise to the Puntacana Resort & Club hotel (where Oscar and Julio would live while their houses were being built) and a small clay runway that allowed the small planes of anyone who dared explore the then secret destination to land.

But to get here, Frank had to experience his own "desert crossing," something that only a person with vision, patience, and an iron will could bear.

The beginnings of Punta Cana were anything but simple. In the mid-1970s, amid the urban project's developmental works, the land was invaded; it began attracting the curiosity of other companies

Above top: The first flights arrived at an unfinished terminal of Punta Cana International Airport.
Above left: Tony Yapor, air operation manager, and José Ramón Fabian, terminal manager, transporting luggage on a small tractor of Club Mediterranée.
Above right: The first flights arrived in 1973. Nine-passenger airplanes of Alas del Caribe airline.

"Everything here works in favor of the people because it's sunny, you can relax, you can reflect, you can think, you have time to really enjoy your life . . . "

Julio Iglesias

Above top: Julio Iglesias and Oscar de la Renta admiring the view of the resort.
Above bottom: Frank Rainieri next to Julio Iglesias and Oscar de la Renta when they went to Punta Cana to show support a few days after Hurricane George in 1998. They organized a musical event.

interested in the work that this small company had started. After a smear campaign and some truly difficult moments, the project's founders understood the importance of finding a prestigious partner to be able to face their challenges. And so in 1978 the then "Punta Cana Club" closed its doors to include on its grounds "Club Mediterranée," the area's first international hotel establishment.

Several years later, in December 1983 and to the bewilderment of local media, the first plane landed. It had nine passengers aboard and landed "in the middle of nowhere," as some of the locals (who could not understand the scope and range of what was to come) dared—quite incorrectly—to assume. The dream was starting to come true. Until that moment, the only way to get to Punta Cana had been an exhausting, hectic, four-hour journey through the jungle or by boat.

In the mid-1990s—1997, if I'm not mistaken—Oscar and Julio joined the company that managed the place. They were only thinking of buying plots for their own houses, but Oscar's natural energy and enthusiasm were transformed into creating a society where friendship and a common vision were fundamental to the development that was to come. Just two years later, Oscar was already beginning to make his undeniable mark on Punta Cana's old golf villas, converting them into the marvelous Tortuga Bay hotel. To this day, Tortuga Bay continues to be as exclusive and atmospheric as on day one.

In the years that followed, they built a series of residential developments together, assigning them names associated with the setting: "Arrecife" ["Coral Reef"], "Hacienda" ["Homestead"], "Tortuga" ["Turtle"], "La Marina" ["The Shore"], "Los Lagos" ["The Lakes"], and "Corales" ["Coral"] were born. This last was where Oscar decided to build his own marvelous home: a house inspired by the neoclassicism of Palladio, with a touch of North American southern plantations, adapted to the area's materials.

The base of the house is Coralina stone—a porous material, the exact color of the sand on the beaches surrounding it, and with a warm texture. A dream built to overwhelm the senses, to fill one with its light, its breezes, and that constant movement of air. So many years of unforgettable memories.

Oscar immediately began to fill his house with friends. There was a continuous passage of people. Christmases, holidays, carnival (which in the Dominican Republic is an explosion of color and beauty), any occasion was the perfect excuse for us to gather within his four friendly walls. In that home we shared a roof, food, dance, and so much laughter and happiness. With friends like Lee Radziwill, Barbara Walters, Joaquín Cortés, Brooke Astor, Bunny Williams, the Clintons, the Kissingers, Mikhail Baryshnikov, Carolina Herrera, Bill Blass, Chessy Rayner, Anna Wintour, Nan Kempner, and so many others, I was spoiled beyond belief by Oscar and his impeccable wife Annette—who is the perfect hostess under any circumstance: she is someone who does not know the meaning of the word "difficult," because for her, doing the impossible is a daily event.

Fashion, of course, was also present in Punta Cana. Color, eclecticism, relaxed elegance—which they have now decided to call "quiet luxury"—was always present throughout our days and nights in Punta Cana.

The dress codes were always relaxed, but there were always rules. For example, at night, Oscar always dressed in meticulous white, in homage to the serenity of the place, but also the joy it inspired. He was proud of his island, his people and their colors . . . All these elements were also present in his fashion collections.

Oscar not only danced beautifully, he also sang! He loved Julio Iglesias's songs and he entertained us with them many a night after a fabulous dinner prepared by the faithful María (with whom he would sometimes launch into dancing merengues!).
María . . . the cook who was Oscar's tireless shadow during his continual intrusions into the kitchens. She was the one responsible for recreating delicious Dominican cooking, never forgetting the *arroz con leche* (rice pudding) that was Oscar's

favorite dessert. She was an extraordinary woman. Not a single detail escaped her; she knew everything.

It is impossible not to talk about the garden. Oscar personally took responsibility for going to the nursery and choosing the plants. Under his guardianship, Sarah Bermudez, a Spanish landscaper, grew the most fantastic orchid garden imaginable.

Or the animals, which Oscar loved and constantly brought in from the streets. Dogs, cats, donkeys . . . any and all animals were possible "victims" of his generosity and affection.

When I arrived in Punta Cana for the first time, it was barely a small town of 4,000 inhabitants. Today, more than 50,000 people live in the area. What was at first a small school with twelve students is today an educational complex with more than one hundred classrooms housing a thousand students. Oscar contributed to this growth not only with his usual energy, but also by building important support centers such as Atención Pediátrica Oscar de la Renta [The Oscar de la Renta Paediatric Care Center] that offers medical services to children five and under. It sees more than 34,000 patients annually and its aid goes directly to economically depressed areas and those who need support the most. It has been several years since Oscar left us, but my reunion with Punta Cana has been like reuniting with my old friend, with someone dear to you that you will always carry in your heart, who makes your life richer, more valuable. To meet Oscar was to fall in love forever with the Dominican Republic, and, therefore, with Punta Cana.

The Houses

Villa Macanao

Year
Completed 2020

Style
Asian tropical

Architects
Antonio Imbert
& Simples Arquitectura

Interior designer
Maria Elmufdi

Landscape designer
Rosangela Bobea

Outdoor features
An exuberant and daring design surrounds the house with exotic corridors of hanging plants and original details of Caribbean architecture. The center of the design is its pool that opens to the sea surrounded by different types of palm trees and fitted with a spacious solarium. The villa is accessed by a spacious porch where visitors are welcomed by a spectacular pool of water.

Villa Macanao is an expression of simple, elegant beauty that honors a magnificent horizon of blue ocean hues and magical tropical light. It leans unobtrusively out in the direction of the sunrise over Playa Serena, and its architectural personality is typical of the Asian tropics. Here, the boundaries between exterior and interior are imperceptible, while water and greenery dance throughout every corner of the home. The villa is designed around a large central pond of varying depths that is interrupted by a spacious gazebo. On both sides, covered walkways connect three blocks of identical bedrooms. These, together with the two main bedrooms and two air-conditioned living rooms facing the beach, complete this villa. As far as nature is concerned, its protagonists are broached stone (the loveliest material in Punta Cana), local Coralina, and Camaru wood. The villa is situated so that it overlooks the sea and features minimal interiors and streamlined, contemporary lines. Nothing superfluous, pretentious, or excessively decorated, in accordance with Imbert's architecture. This was achieved through the use of organic materials, whitewashed wood, neutral colors, and smooth textures. The joinery work of the ceilings, facing, and bespoke furniture plays a leading role. A spectacular entry through the grand foyer receives visitors with a set of artisan-made wicker lanterns. The focal point from this entryway is the living room, which frames a spectacular view of the incomparable Punta Cana coastline.

Villa Las Brisas

Year
Completed 2010

Style
Plantation

Architects
Zorrilla & Baquero Arquitectos

Interior designer
Monica Damonte

Landscape designer
Jesús Ibáñez

Outdoor features
The spacious garden features several areas with varied styles and Tuscan inspiration. A pool of water was placed at the entrance, flanked by geometric flower beds and date palms. The guest house is tucked into a spacious palm grove and has a pebble-paved courtyard that forms original motifs. The part facing the sea is a large meadow that can be used in many ways. It is surrounded by the green waves of undulating flower beds. The house's large pool is entirely exposed to the turquoise sea and decorated with several wooden pergolas, large coconut trees, and blue-flowered climbing plants.

This compound was developed as a world of courtyards. Each one has a different theme, inviting visitors to discover the variety of finished environments.
With the idea of experiencing the house from the outside, arches were built on the first floor to enjoy the sitting areas while appreciating the majesty of the Caribbean Sea and the greenness of the golf course. The second floor, where the views are more spectacular, has the main living room and private spaces, like bedrooms and studies. These are bordered by a series of Tuscan columns made from Coralina stone, which support a unique ceiling, designed entirely of wood. The interior of the house features high ceilings and large picture windows that allow natural light to flood each room.
The original idea for the villa's interior came from Oscar de la Renta. The architectural model is obviously "Palladian," beautifully made for Señor de la Renta's niece.
The selected colors were carefully studied so that they might bring more light from the outside inside, in a relaxed, natural way to make each environment feel warmer. For the external room, only one color was used: "sage green." The wall of the living-dining room, in neoclassical style, is adorned with light-reflecting ceramic tiles made by Portuguese artisans. The reception room on the first floor reminds us of "Chinoiserie"; the fabrics have an Eastern influence, in accordance with Oscar de la Renta's original design.

Outside, there is another reception area where a pool table can be found. The *losanghe* parquet is quite reminiscent of Havana's colonial halls. The furniture was custom-made from Damonte Studio designs with colonial inspiration. Furniture and objects are from the South of France and Italy, which complete the common and family areas.

Villa Las Arenas

Year
Completed 2004

Style
Palladian classic

Architects
Juanchy Zorrilla and Trini Baquero (Zorrilla & Baquero Arquitectos)

Interior designers
Jane Taylor and Serena Balfour

Landscape designer
Sarah Bermúdez

Outdoor features
An elegant garden with a large pool and paths lined by royal palms on both sides. The home has several terraces decorated with large planters made from Coralina and Areca. At the villa's entrance, an orderly courtyard has been designed with geometric shapes and two fountains facing each other.

Surrounded by a coupled-column colonnade, this house is enlarged by the proportion of its spaces and details, making clear reference to fifteenth-century colonial residences in the Americas.
It is built of stone columns and walls and is made up of a central block containing the family's bedrooms and leisure spaces plus two wings that frame the front courtyard. These are shaded by beautiful almond trees, which provide visual protection and create a unique atmosphere for the entryway.
Several symbolic materials—such as the brickwork in the courtyards, combined with Coralina, green shutters, arched doorways, and architectural details like moldings and mosaic floors—provide a touch of historic charm and more clearly demonstrate the traditional composition the architects referenced.
Much of the furniture is custom-made in Vietnam, while the soft furnishings were produced exclusively in the Dominican Republic.

Johannes Vermeer

THE COLONIAL ANDES

Villa Corales 7

Year
Completed 1998

Style
Veranda house

Architect
Ernesto Buch

Interior designer
Oscar de la Renta

Landscape designer
Oscar de la Renta

Outdoor features
The garden carries the unmistakable stamp of Oscar de la Renta, both in its line and ornamental details. Elegant, serious, orderly, and with a clearly tropical accent. Different environments are bound together with long paths shaded by local trees, royal poincianas, and coconuts, with dense and natural lateral vegetation. The home's entrance has a private chapel and huge flowerpots where cheerful white bougainvillea and trimmed ficus grow. The sea can be seen from every part of the garden, and its breeze reaches every corner, filling the air with freshness. Fountains, ponds, and gazebos complement this unique and special garden.

This was the first house built in the new Punta Cana Corales development. In search of inspiration, Louisiana plantation houses and their use of terraces were researched. Houses with verandas are especially well-suited to the Caribbean climate; in fact, examples of houses with terraces are found on many of the islands. Deep terraces protect the house from sun and rain, as well as offer living room areas that are covered but open-air, lovely in this warm but windy climate prone to intense sunlight and sudden downpours.
The house's main floor is on the upper level. Opposite the front porch are stone pillars and tall, slender wooden posts, reminiscent of classic raised Creole cottages.
The double staircases lead to an upper loggia, which opens directly through glazed doors into a spacious living room. From there, twin doors lead to a terrace overlooking the sea. The bedrooms are accessed from this terrace. At ground level, an open-air passageway leads to the lower terrace, where there are additional bedrooms and a patio that provides a framed view of the sea.
The front façade is to scale with its esplanade, while the façade that overlooks the sea is to a bigger scale and can be seen from the ocean. On this façade, double-height Tuscan columns made of Coralina support the ceiling and the floor of the upper gallery. The house is made of concrete, while the roof structure is made of wood. The roofing material is

composed of cedar shingles and the walls are lined with Coralina. There is extensive carpentry work with classical details (like cornices and skirting boards) as well as door and window architraves made of locally crafted, high-quality wood.

REMBRANDT
WORLD ARCHITECTURE

THE SIBLEY GUIDE TO BIRDS
The Great Naturalists
On Distant Shores OVIDIO GUAITA

CENTURY

Gunnera manicata

Villa Corales 50

Year
Completed 2015

Style
Spanish colonial

Architects
Juanchy Zorrilla and Trini Baquero
(Zorrilla & Baquero Arquitectos)

Interior designers
Hamilton South and Manuel Bellod

Landscape designer
Rosangela Bobea

Outdoor features
A comfortable garden that is organized around the porch and large Coralina pool. As a central element, a triple-spouted, Italian Renaissance-style wall fountain stands out, surrounded by small hedges trimmed with green island ficus.

This house lies on a small hill in the second row from the sea. Its positioning is due to a quest for views and diverse colors that the Caribbean Sea offers, recalling the Spanish colonials that inspired it.
The masonry arches surrounding its social areas accentuate the house's romantic character. These, alongside the use of materials and appropriate proportion management, highlight the architectural charm. Upon entering this Spanish colonial-style residence, one notes the spacious foyer, with its double Coralina-stone staircases and wooden handrails, and its corridors developed in an open and fluid way. The details of traditional elements (covered, open-air terraces; high-ceilinged living rooms; the simple yet exquisitely decorated spaces) join the stone paths and sound of water in fountains, accentuating the central concept and inviting one to live outside, next to gardens characterized by the area's typical lush vegetation.
It is precisely this combination of elements that makes this a home to enjoy all year round.
Nearly all the furniture was purchased at auctions and antiques shops in Spain, the UK, and the US. The fabrics are primarily by Le Manach and Carolina Irving. Many of the objects inside the house were gifts from the owners' dear friends: Annette and Oscar de la Renta, from their house in Santo Domingo; and Lee Radziwill, from her house in Paris.

CENTURY
RALPH LAUREN
AFRICAN FORMS

Villa Corales 8

Year
Completed 2002

Style
Beach colonial hacienda

Architect
Juan Montoya

Interior designer
Juan Montoya

Landscape designers
Tony Costa and Ana Portella
Costa Nursery Farms

Outdoor features
Design with a colonial accent thanks to a fresh, leafy central courtyard. The architecture of the house maintains a close relationship with the garden, which, at all times, aims to seduce with its innovative layout and peculiar sea front. Various types of palm trees, large-leaved plants, and green tapestries are the basis of the design. The Coralina pool is an extension of the ocean into the house.

This large Spanish Mexican-inspired house is reminiscent of the big Latin American haciendas that use an albero yellow on their exteriors. This house is designed around a series of central courtyards, crossed by wooden bridges. Here, lush vegetation and a small stream have been introduced, integrating nature into the building's interior.
The house's carpentry plays a large architectural (as well as decorative) role. A very dark hue is used in the courtyards' interior structures to form bridges and perimeter mezzanines that unite the two parts of the building. Externally, it is a very solid building; inside it is highly permeable with the central courtyard garden opening onto a large living room and porch that overlooks the pool, beach, and sea. Here the concept of interior and exterior is blurred. Elements of military architecture seen in Spanish forts have also been used—in this case, to build an outdoor, sea-facing terrace made of large stone blocks. Inside are ceilings with exposed dark wood beams; the exterior albero color is introduced into the living room and common areas with a rustic plastering base.
Its decoration is also dominated by dark wooden furniture with white cotton canvas upholstery, all of which gives an air of great sobriety and austerity to the space. The selected artwork stands out by adding color and freshness. Most of these pieces are by South American artists such as Botero and Guayasamín. To finish the decoration, a series of

artisanal objects as well as several exotic pieces (such as African sculptures) were chosen. This is all surrounded by exuberant tropical vegetation, arranged naturally so that the building's monumental character is somewhat softened by the introduction of vegetation inside.

DESIGNING PARAD
PUNTA CANA
Arquitectura Natural
Kevin Fleming The Heart of

HARINA
ARROZ
PASTAS

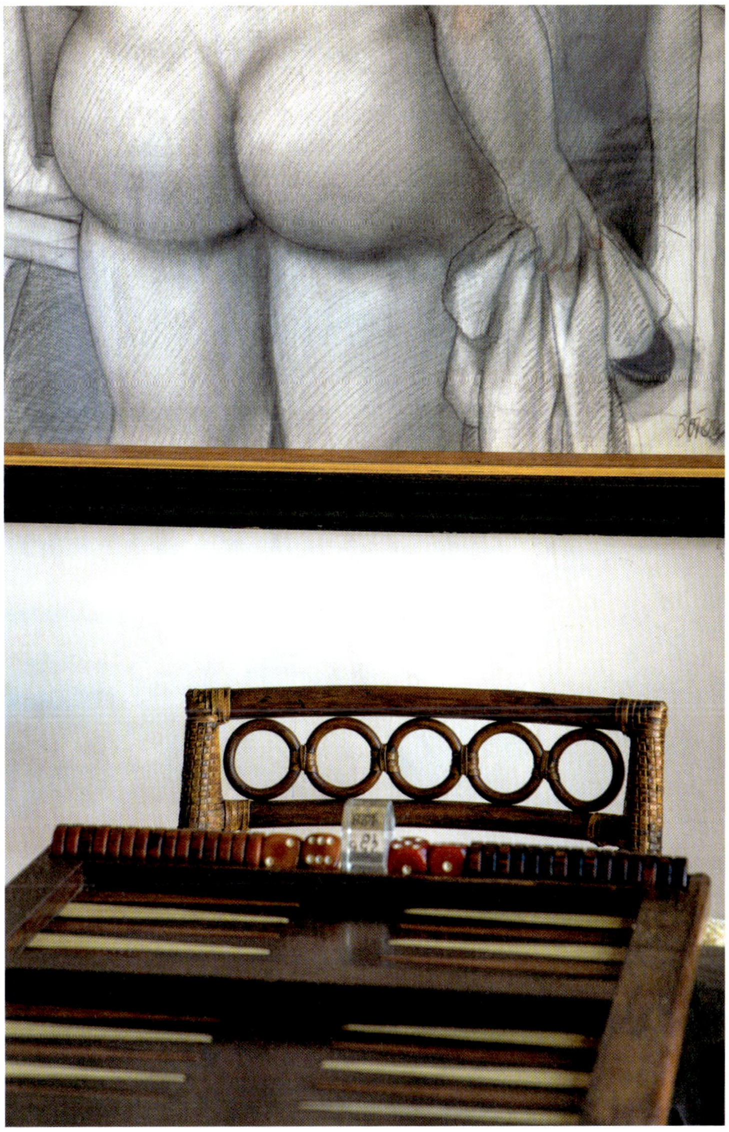

Villa Alta Gracia

Year
Completed 2018

Style
Colonial Caribbean-inspired

Architects
Mario and Janet Desangles

Interior designers
Agence Moinard Betaille
with Corinne Lantenois

Landscape designer
Rosangela Bobea

Outdoor features
Views of the Corales golf course are this simple and unpretentious garden's essence. The native trees that surround the house have been respected to their fullest, combined with new vegetation of palm trees and giant leafy shrubs. Everywhere there are palm tree trunks sprouting with vividly colored and fragrant orchids.

Located in Corales, Puntacana Resort, this nostalgic, classic, and traditional villa is developed on a large plot of land with stunning views of the golf course. Despite having a certain formality, this house is characterized by its large doors and windows that allow in abundant light and fluidity, connecting the interior and exterior. The central entrance is for pedestrians only and upon passing through the gate, visitors discover the beauty of its colonial-style architecture, being surrounded by two fountains and lush vegetation.

The house's formal entrance consists of a reception area with a large basket arch and white-painted oak doorways. This reception area leads into an interior garden, and it connects the entire house through corridors formed by successions of arches and wooden pergolas.

The house is symmetrical and made up of two blocks, each of which consists of three spaces. The first single-story block forms the service units on both sides, whose spaces are kept to a smaller scale, while the formal entrance is in the center.

The second block accommodates all the other areas of the house—the first floor contains the living rooms, dining room, terraces, kitchen, with bedrooms on the first and second floors. As is typical of colonial houses, the interior courtyard is designed as a space that organizes the different rooms of the house. It allows the breeze to circulate and light to enter, creating a pleasant outdoor-living feeling.

The series of arches, high ceilings, galleries, and balconies contribute to the colonial style of the villa, as does the use of light and natural stone (coral and limestone) on the floors and walls.

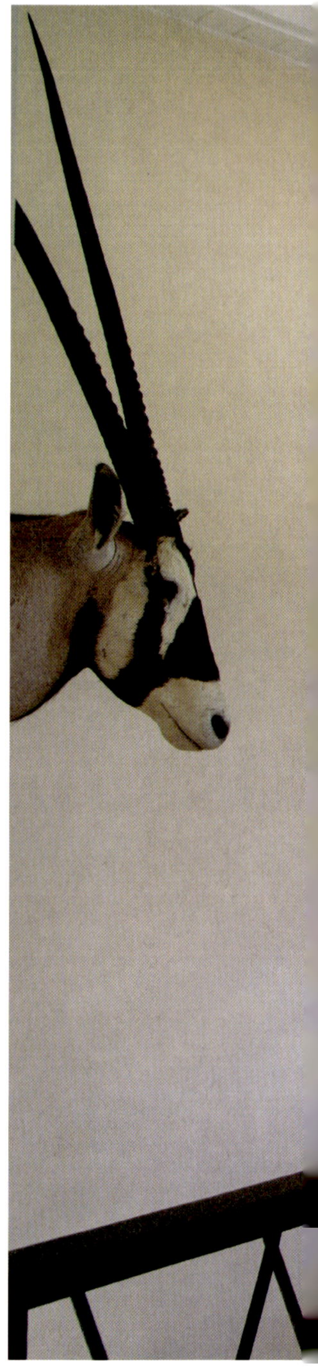

La Confusa Bendecida

Year
Completed 1998

Style
Tropical vernacular

Architect
Oscar Imbert Tessón

Interior designer
Oscar Imbert Tessón

Landscape designer
Oscar Imbert Tessón

Outdoor features
Exotic, daring, and wild: such is this garden nestled on the coast, in perfect harmony with its surroundings and Oscar Imbert's peculiar architecture. The wooden corridors are filled with natural life: lianas, palms, and native trees. The seeming disorder is captivating right from the start, thanks to its originality and ever-present birdsong.

One finds the structure of La Confusa Bendecida immersed in a tropical forest typical of the area. This house is built with all local materials: eucalyptus logs and a thatched roof. It is a clear example of tropical vernacular architecture where nature and the vast Caribbean Sea, with its turquoise waters and white sand, are the framework for this tropical paradise.

Designed by architect Oscar Imbert, whose projects include the Punta Cana airport and whose residential designs are today considered the symbol of Punta Cana, La Confusa Bendecida is a spectacular example of green and sustainable architecture. The house has a central snail-shaped structure off of which the living areas have been built. Everything is connected by bridges and walkways, creating a uniquely designed space.

La Confusa has a central living room with two open rooms to fit a large number of guests and a dining room with a central table and two side tables.

There are four bedrooms with en suite bathrooms and a study that can convert into a bedroom.

The house faces the sea and has immediate access to the beach and the beautiful springs that have existed since the Taíno era and which are now protected.

Villa La Colina

Year
Completed 2006

Style
Caribbean Palladian

Architect
Ernesto Buch

Interior designer
Bunny Williams

Landscape designer
Bunny Williams

Outdoor features
Shade is the basis for this exotic and surprising garden. Different linked environments and living areas are strung together throughout the garden. Ornamental details surprise at every turn, hidden among the lush vegetation or sometimes as central parts of more orderly spaces. The large Arecas provide shade and intimacy in much of the space while at the same time providing a pleasant feeling of freshness.

With definite similarity to the previous houses in Punta Cana, precedents and typologies that respond well to this warm but windy climate were sought out. Among these, the veranda house is especially suitable. Verandas not only protect the inside of the house from sun and rain, but they also provide shaded open-air living rooms.

Outdoor living rooms, such as terraces and loggias, are widely used. This house is built on an oceanfront property, which can be appreciated from the other side of the street. The rear of the property borders on a golf course and a meadow, and it has the highest elevation in the area. The house is also located at the back of the property, on the highest ground, to enjoy the sea views to their fullest.

The house is accessed by a path lined with palm trees along one side. The path goes up a gentle slope and reaches a courtyard located behind the house. The entrance is found at the back, which overlooks the courtyard, and is thus the front of the house. The double semicircular, floating stairs lead to a pedimented loggia with Tuscan columns on the upper level, the main floor. The upper loggia rests on a rustic base with arched openings, part of the lower loggia. The upper loggia leads directly to a centrally located living room, which opens on the opposite side to a wraparound terrace with a panoramic view of the sea. The high vaulted ceiling and large openings on opposite sides allow the sea breeze to enter. The tall white columns of the upper

SWIMMING POOL
AQUATIC LIFE
living in Sri Lanka
EUROPE IN THE MIDDLE AGES

veranda are superimposed on the lower veranda's rustic Tuscan pillars. Local materials were selected for the house's interior. These include native stones, like Coraline, widely used for floors; locally quarried limestone; and fieldstone. For the bathroom floors, cement or mosaic tiles were used.

These floor tiles—which are available in a variety of colors and patterns—became popular in the nineteenth century in much of the Caribbean (where they are still manufactured) and parts of Latin America. The exterior wall finish is *perrilla* crushed limestone, which does not require painting. Its color varies from white-wash to cream-beige, depending on the color of the stone. The surfaces of the walls are beige in color. The columns are white, with a smooth finish.

John GRISHAM
THE MAN WHO RAN
WASHINGTON
NUREYEV
SLAND HOTEL STORIES
WILLIAM BECKFORD
ONE MAN'S FOLLY
GEROME

LEE CHILD
TOM GRACE
Henning Mankell
BEAT THE REAPER

Death Comes to Pemberley
P. D. James
Ian McEwan
Atonement
The Shadow Girls
Penelope Lively
SHANTARAM
Patti Smith
Lisa Wingate
Tending Roses
The Titled Americans
LOVING FRANK
SHIRLEY HAZZARD
Frankie's Place
Objects of Desire
WATER for ELEPHANTS

CARIBBEAN STYLE
Lewis and Clark

Casa Playa Grande

Year
Completed 1999

Style
Caribbean Palladian

Architect
Rhina López Marranzini

Interior designers
Oscar de la Renta
and Aurorita de la Rocha

Landscape designer
Sarah Bermúdez

Outdoor features
A garden with large spaces and several living areas. The entrance to the villa is presided over by a circular pond beneath the shade of date palms and flowering feather trees. An elegant pergola, loaded with blue thunbergia flowers, guides us toward the house, where the sea suddenly appears in the background. On the main terrace, next to the pool, what stand out are the undulating wave-shaped flowerbeds and the free-growing forest of coconut trees on the sand of the private beach.

The design of this villa, whose construction was completed in 1999, thoroughly conforms to the owners' requirements: its open, spacious rooms aim to create the best views of the Caribbean Sea, taking advantage of the sun and breeze; the layout separates social spaces from private ones; the style is traditional, with tropical elements and precious materials.
Everything stems from a longitudinal walkway, which runs parallel to the sea. Here is where all the units scattered among the gardens emerge. The original structure had three main units, each with sea views and natural ventilation. The shared section has an extensive living room on a double-height single level, entirely surrounded by terraces. To the front, an infinity pool seamlessly joins this space with the sea. When it comes time to set the table, one can choose between a dining room that is part of the walkway, one that is completely open-air, or one that has air-conditioning but can be completely opened, with its wood and glass doors. The private unit has five bedrooms: three on the first floor and two on the second. The family living room is on the second floor. The kitchen, laundry, and service rooms create the indispensable support unit. More units were later added using design parameters and materials identical to the originals: a guest cabana was built with two rooms, a gym, and a new service area. And, on the beach, a gazebo with a built-in kitchen was installed: a place of

interaction between the beach and a space where informal gatherings between family and friends can be organized.
Among the materials, the ones that stand out are the concrete in the structures and the precious materials like the wood and tiles on the ceilings or the Coralina stone and wooden flooring. The columns are covered with Coralina stone and the bathrooms, with marble. The interior design work is structured in simple, straightforward lines; the clean use of wood to apply colors to the walls without detracting from the beauty that surrounds us. The blue of the sea on one side and the green

nature on the other combine to form part of the decoration. The combination of elements and decorative pieces, which were acquired on trips around the world, adds a touch of eclecticism to the house, without overloading it or even competing with its original style.

Villa Corales 21

Year
Completed 2000

Style
Caribbean Palladian

Architects
Ernesto Buch and
Zorrilla & Baquero Arquitectos

Interior designer
Niobe Robles

Landscape designer
Sarah Bermúdez

Outdoor features
An orderly and sober garden, with architectural elements in harmony with the elegant architecture. Two symmetrical ponds adorned with lush tropical vegetation welcome visitors to the villa. Tall phoenix palms are the stars of this generous space. In the garden's living area, the blue sea takes a leading role next to proud coconut trees.

This magnificent complex, which is located on the reef within the exclusive Coral section of Punta Cana, was created by the firm Zorrilla & Baquero in partnership with architect Ernesto Buch.
A source of inspiration for the design of this house was the English, who brought their version of Palladian architecture to the Caribbean. They adapted it to the warm and sunny climate of these islands—very different from the climate of the British Isles.
The development of this project was based on compositional freedom paired with the classical model's precepts of the original Palladian styles. These were characterized by their elegance and symmetry and the use of sea views.
The house consists of a two-story main villa with an explicitly Palladian look. There are two-story porches on opposite sides. One side faces the sea; the other, the entrance courtyard. The porticos are trisected. Four coral stone columns on the upper floor have Tuscan profiles but Roman-Doric proportions. At ground level, there are Tuscan pillars beneath each column, each pair framing an arch and creating a classical Roman motif. The roof is made up of wooden shingles that are widely used throughout the English-speaking isles.
This family home is essentially developed on one floor, except for the main wing, which is developed on two levels. The first floor contains a spectacular living room with a wealth of unparalleled materials:

Coralina walls, wooden floors, and plaster formwork ceilings. This level is supplied with tall windows that allow one to enjoy the beauty of the coastal setting and the sea breeze. The main suite has been developed on the upper floor. Additionally, two one-story structures can be seen in front and to either side of the main villa. These stand as *barchesse*, defining the two sides of an entrance courtyard. One is a study/video room while the other is a large

dining room. The kitchen, in a separate space, is connected to the dining room by a covered hallway. The villa is surrounded by gardens that are a true paradise: fountains, cobbled paths, fruit-bearing and aromatic plants.

THE ART OF LIVING

HOTELS
CALATRAVA

Villa Marina 24

Year
Completed 2022

Style
Mediterranean

Architect
Genevieve F. Markesinis

Interior designer
Genevieve F. Markesinis

Landscape designer
Genevieve F. Markesinis

Outdoor features
Dutch-inspired house with an arid garden where agaves and succulents play leading roles. The meadow has been replaced by earthy areas made with beach sand and rocks. In the pool, the palma cana makes its scenic, shady appearance next to the other low-maintenance plants with grayish tones.

This house is perhaps the most personal one presented in this book. It was designed by its owner and built by local tradesmen. Its proportions are quite small and restrained, moving away from an enormous structure, and conveying instead a more relaxed, comfortable soul.

The owner was inspired by tropical, Asian, and Caribbean architecture, using rustic wood and thatched roofs and introducing elements of vernacular Mediterranean architecture. There are also clear references to colonial Dutch architecture, as in the case of the main façade.

The architectural structure of the house is developed around a large cylindrical central space crowned by a large conical roof. This serves as an arrival and gathering point, while at the same time radially distributing the house's circulation to other rooms.

The decoration of this house is the architecture itself, in which much of the furniture, including the living room's large central sofa, is made of white stonework. A large console that presides over the living room is also stonework and perfectly integrated into the architecture. This merging of furniture with the building, uniting the interior and exterior with a continuous Coralina floor, and the same stone on several key walls, gives great cohesion overall.

This central space is flanked by two other protruding rectangular spaces that are connected to the pool by pergolas. This creates an interesting dialogue between the architecture and the pool, which is marked off by a series of masonry arches with dry stone Coralina walls.

Villa Serena 6

Year
Completed 2019

Style
Modern tropical

Architects
Mareines & Patalano

Interior designers
Mareines & Patalano,
and Jean Pierre Santoni of Basi Co.
(Puerto Rico)

Landscape designers
Rosangela Bobea & Marita Mareines

Outdoor features
The house's avant-garde architecture has a garden along the same lines: bold and original. It has several defined environments with green walkways, vertical gardens, and indoor ponds. Above the building, proud royal palm trees stand out, along with local ground cover plants, ferns, hearts of palm, and coonties.

An open-air house facing the beautiful Caribbean landscape. A house where the idea of inside-out is constantly being questioned. The blue-green waters of the Caribbean Sea merge with the fresh, fish-and-plant-filled waters of an impressive garden. A clear example of avant-garde organic architecture.
The large terrace winds around the entire length of the house. It is a 7,500 ft^2 walk across interior and exterior moods, highs and lows, the most diverse shapes and landscapes, in all directions.
The north block contains six completely independent suites, each with its own view and garden. In the south block we find a dining room, bar, kitchen, games room, and gym, as well as the service areas of the house. In the center of the house, the living room is encased in a modern glass cylinder floating in the middle of the water gardens. The entire double-curved, glue-laminated wood structure (terrace deck and suites) was digitally made in France, as were the steel pillars that support it.
The glass window frames and copper roof with standing seams were made in Spain.
The windowpanes and sheet metal needed for the assembly's perfect tightness and thermal insulation come from the United States. The terrain was raised 6.5 ft from its original height with compacted caliche to prevent the area from flooding in case of a hurricane. On top of finding the perfect placement and construction method for the concrete foundations and walls supporting the steel and wood

structures, no detail was overlooked. This is evident in the artistic quality of the stone, wood, and copper finishes that dominate the aesthetic composition of this house.

KNOB
CREEK

Acknowledgments

Thanks to all the homeowners and their unwavering support, as well as Naty Abascal, Guido Taroni, Anna Wintour, Haydée Rainieri, the Rainieri family, Giancarlo Beras-Goico, Odalis Lugo, Junior Solano, Luis Migoya, Manuel Sajour, Paola Rainieri, and the entire team at Grupo Puntacana and Rizzoli.

Photographs
Guido Taroni

Art Direction and Layout
Giulia Dolci

Translation
Leah Tanaka

Distributed in English throughout the World
by Rizzoli International Publications Inc.
300 Park Avenue South
New York, NY 10010, USA

ISBN: 978-88-918400-5-9

2024 2025 2026 2027 / 10 9 8 7 6 5 4 3 2 1

First edition: April 2024

This volume was printed at Errestampa S.r.l.
Via Portico 27, Orio al Serio, Bergamo
Printed in Italy

Visit us online:
Facebook.com/RizzoliNewYork
Twitter: @Rizzoli_Books
Instagram.com/RizzoliBooks
Pinterest.com/RizzoliBooks
Youtube.com/user/RizzoliNY
Issuu.com/Rizzoli